C000061286

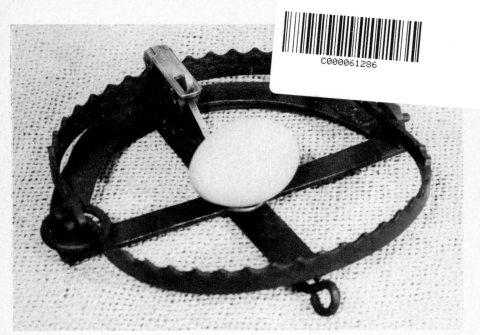

An egg trap, an ingenious trap devised to be held in the set position by the weight of a hen's egg. Only when the egg is removed do the jaws spring shut. It was used against foxes and members of the crow family.

TRAPPING AND POACHING

Arthur Ingram

Shire Publications Ltd

CONTENTS

Printed in Great Britain by C. I. Thomas & Sons (Haverfordwest) Ltd, Press Buildings, Merlins Bridge, Haverfordwest.

NOTE

In this book the author endeavours to record a facet of social history and does not advocate or condone the use of any of the devices or methods described.

The use of steel-toothed or gin-type traps was made illegal in 1958 by the Spring Traps Approval Order. The taking of songbirds is prohibited under the Protection of Birds Acts 1954 and 1967 except by those specifically licensed to do so. Copies of both Acts are obtainable from Her Majesty's Stationery Office.

Badger tongs (see page 28).

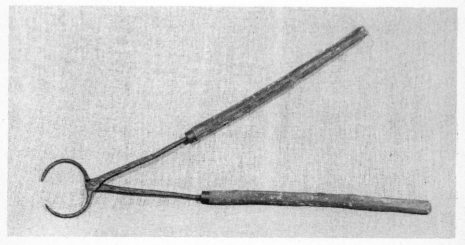

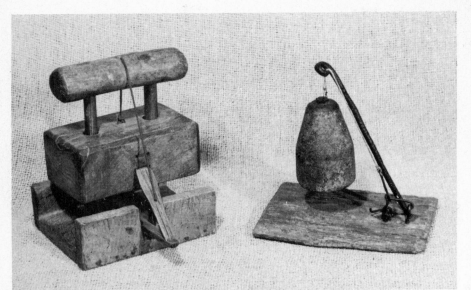

Two deadfall mousetraps: (left) an early nineteenth-century type using a heavy block of oak; (right) an early eighteenth-century example employing a 5½ lb (2.59kg) lead weight.

INTRODUCTION

Traps were among man's earliest innovations, existing alongside his crude flint tools some three hundred thousand years ago. Man, the predator, could not fly to catch the birds of the air, or swim sufficiently well to catch aquatic prey. Most of the terrestrial animals he pursued were either swifter, more agile or more powerful than himself. Man's only great advantages were his wit, cunning and ability to reason. These he gradually applied to observing the behaviour of animals and developing ways of inveigling them into devices he had prepared for their capture. The earliest traps were merely natural features of the landscape such as bogs and chasms into which animals were driven, often with the aid of grass or brush fires. Camouflaged pits around known watering holes and heavy logs or boulders propped over well-used game trails and triggered to fall on unsuspecting quarry gradually evolved. From these humble beginnings sprang the multifarious traps and ingenious devices described in this book.

Poaching arose as a consequence of the affluence of the rich landowners. For them, by Norman times, hunting had ceased to be an essential for survival and had become a sport. They decreed that the wildlife on their land was theirs to the preclusion of the peasant classes. However, an empty stomach and an empty purse have a way of compelling a man to fill them; the harsh penalties were disregarded and poaching became an accepted way of life for very many countrymen. The proficient poacher was both hunter and hunted and lived by his wits. He read the woods and fields in which he walked almost as we might read a book, and failure to do so could mean not only the escape of his intended quarry but also his capture by gamekeeper or warden. The poacher used many of the traps to be described, but because his operations were clandestine he evolved many other devices and cunning ruses, which are also recorded here.

The text does not describe modern types of trap, nor does it cover hunting, shooting or angling, which are subjects in their own right.

3

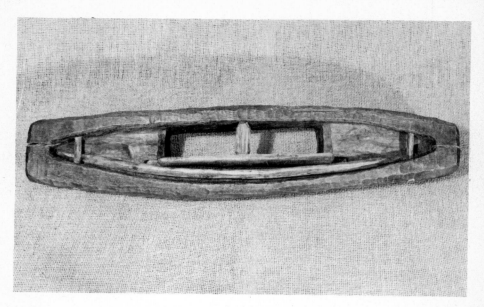

ABOVE: *A treadle deer trap, viewed from below, showing the willow-bow spring forced back by the ash-wood valve, held open by a trigger peg. The deer's foot entered the aperture from the anterior side, dislodging the peg.*

BELOW *(from left to right): Two poacher's throwing sticks; a gamekeeper's truncheon known as a swingle; a blackthorn cudgel used for killing rabbits caught in a long net.*

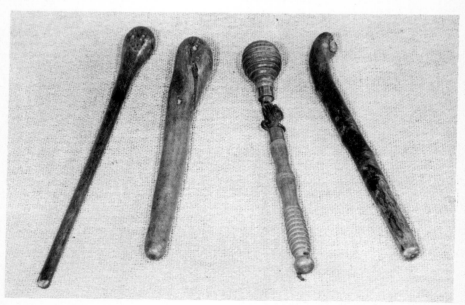

DEER

Probably the earliest of our indigenous animals to be denied to the diet of the common man was the deer. Vast tracts of land were designated as royal hunting forests; to protect these arbitrarily imposed rights William the Conqueror imposed the death penalty for the killing of a royal deer, and all deer at that time were by definition considered royal. This penalty was rescinded by Henry III, but the deer has continued to be strongly protected by landowners up to the present day, although feral deer in certain areas are now considered by farmers as pests.

One of the earliest traps for catching deer has been found preserved in peat bogs in Scotland, Wales, Ireland and eastern Europe and is called a *treadle trap*. Basically it is a heavy log, usually of oak, between 2 feet 6 inches and 5 feet long (760 to 1520mm) with an aperture some 9 inches by 4 inches (230 by 100mm) cut in its centre. At its base it is hollowed to a concave groove almost the width of the log and approximately 2 inches (50mm) deep. A flat wooden 'valve' was crudely hinged into the aperture, opening downwards, and was held open by a wooden peg. This forced the valve back against a willow bow which was housed in the concave base. The trap was then in the set position and was placed in a shallow camouflaged pit on a well-used trail. A deer placing its foot through the aperture at the top would dislodge the peg, allowing the valve to snap shut under pressure from the willow bow, trapping the foot between the valve and the body of the trap. The trap was not secured but the weight of it impeded the deer so that it could be overtaken and killed. This type of trap was in use from the bronze age possibly until post-Roman times. Deer were also hunted with spear and bow and were caught in camouflaged pit traps in early times.

When deer became protected, poachers found other ways of taking them. Dogs of many types were used to drag down and often kill them. Snares which looped around either neck or fetlock were common. Large tree bowls, propped on branchwood so that the slightest pressure on the trigger mechanism, liberally baited with grain, brought it crashing down on the victim's back, were also used; these were known as *deadfall traps*. Shooting was also practised by some, as it was in the poaching of all animals, but the sound of a shot ringing through the woods would obviously alert the gamekeeper, so the accomplished poacher rarely resorted to it, especially with deer, as one could not quickly make one's escape when hampered by the weight of a deer carcase.

Not only poachers but also wealthy medieval landowners trapped deer. This was to increase the numbers stocking their well-managed deer parks. The trap was called a *deer leap* or *deer dyke*. It consisted of a wide ditch and a bank topped by a low wooden fence, and it formed part of the perimeter fence of the park. The ditch was about 6 feet (1.8m) deep and 12 feet (3.7m) wide. The bank and fence, about 3 feet (0.9m) high overall, ran outside this. In winter grain was scattered in the ditch, enticing wild deer to leap over the low fence and so tumble down into the ditch, whose depth and width made the return jump to freedom impossible.

RABBITS AND HARES

The hare is indigenous to the British Isles, but the rabbit was introduced, possibly by the Romans, but more probably by the Normans. The rabbit has attracted the attention of poachers more than any other creature, and a great variety of devices has been employed against it. From medieval times until the late nineteenth century rabbits were carefully managed as a source of meat. Most estates employed a warrener to tend the rabbit colonies — hence the surname Warren. The rabbit was looked upon by countryfolk as the ideal animal for the pot.

The most commonly used method of taking rabbits was the *snare,* simply a loop usually of copper or brass wire. Although a device of the simplest construction, it required a great degree of skill in setting. It was set in a well-used run through a hedge or tall grass. The run of a rabbit has a set pattern, the form of which was critical in setting a successful snare. The rabbit progresses in long and short hops, always landing in the same spots on the run; these spots are clearly defined to the practised eye by the compression of the grass and are known as squats. The rabbit stops to look about after long hops but does not tarry on the short hop. The snare is placed just behind the short hop squat. The snare is attached to a wooden peg driven into the ground, held in position by a second, smaller, cleft-top peg known as the teeler, so that the bottom of the loop is four fingers' width from the ground. This is calculated to snare the rabbit around the neck as it springs forward from the squat.

There are two variations on this: in the first the snare is attached to a pegged-down sapling, which catapults the rabbit into the air when it is sprung; in the second, the snare is attached to a stick some 3 feet (900mm) in length. When snared, the rabbit is not restrained but can pull the stick with it until it reaches its burrow, where the stick becomes jammed across the entrance. When the operator visits the warren he can see the sticks and pull the snared rabbits from their burrows.

Another type of trap used against the rabbit was the ubiquitous steel-toothed or *gin trap*. This was a steel trap consisting of a pair of serrated jaws, usually about 4 inches (100mm) long for rabbits, hinged at the bottom to lie flat and open like a gaping mouth, and held in this position by the flat trigger platform. Thus positioned, the jaws held down the metal spring arm, which was about 5 inches (130mm) long and riveted to an extension of the base. When a rabbit trod on the trigger plate the jaws were released and forced rapidly upwards in an arc by the depressed spring to clamp tightly around the victim's leg. These traps were secured by a chain and sturdy iron peg and used in a variety of situations; perhaps the commonest was partly to bury it at the entrance of the burrow. To do this the poacher carried with him a special short-handled *trapper's hammer*. The head had at one end a

hammer face for knocking in the iron pegs and at the other a broad flat blade for scooping out the soil to bury the trap. The term *gin trap* is thought to be derived from the word *engine*, which at one time was used to describe any device that worked independently of man. Most traps do this but the term seems to have become synonymous with the steel-toothed ones.

Nets were often used to catch rabbits; these were either long nets or gate nets. *Long nets* could be as long as the poacher wanted but were normally around 100 feet (30m) in length and 3 feet (0.9m) in height; they were made of twisted hemp or flax and of 2¼-inch (57mm) mesh. This net was placed across the face of a rabbit warren on a night when the rabbits were out feeding upwind. A night when moonlight was periodically blackened by scudding clouds was considered ideal for long-netting. The poacher would remain concealed, planning the laying of his net, until a cloud darkened the sky; then he would stealthily creep out and lay a few yards of net, carefully pegging it upright on light wooden poles and ensuring there was plenty of slack to entangle the rabbits. Just as the cloud was completing its passage over the moon he would conceal himself again, plan his next stage and wait for another cloud. This process was repeated until the whole length was laid. The poacher then sent out his dog in a wide arc to come in behind the rabbits. Their headlong flight was sharply arrested as they became enmeshed in the net. The poacher then needed to hurry along the length of the net dispatching the rabbits with a cudgel before they broke away. A favourite ploy of keepers to prevent warrens being long-netted was to scatter branches of blackthorn or briars about it. These became entangled in the net when it was being gathered up and made the operation almost impossible. The poacher might get one bag of rabbits but he could ill afford the net he would lose as a result.

Gate nets were similar to long nets but normally had a 2-inch (50mm) mesh and measured 12 feet by 4 feet (3.7m by 1.2m) to hang on a five-bar field-gate. The poacher's dog was again sent around behind the rabbit, which almost always would head for the gate to make good its escape — only to find the poacher's hands

'Setting a hare snare', from 'The Gamekeeper at Home', 1878.

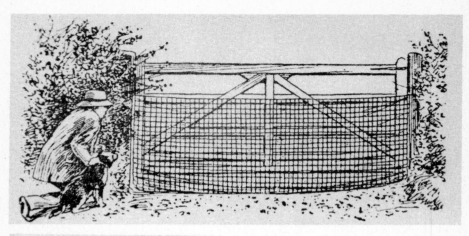

(124) SPRING FERRET MUZZLES.

Improved. Can be put on with one hand, and cannot work loose. **6d.** each ; **3/6** dozen ; **2/-** ½ dozen.

(126) NEW IMPROVED HUMANE HINGED FERRET MUZZLE.

Silver Plated. Best Muzzle on Market. Very light. No projections. Cannot catch in roots, &c. **10d.** each ; **8/6** dozen. **4/6** ½ doz.

(127) BRASS FERRET MUZZLES.

With adjustable bar to fit any size Ferret, **4½d.** each ; **1/6** six, **2/6** doz. Post free.

(128) FERRET BELLS AND COLLARS.

Hand-made, strong Leather, **8d.** each. 3, **1/8**. **BELLS 3d.**, Three, **7d.**, **1/6** per doz. ½ dozen, **1/-**. Post Free.

ABOVE: *A poacher and his dog concealed in readiness behind a gate net set for a hare.*

LEFT: *An advertisement for ferreting accessories from an early catalogue issued by a Dorset firm specialising in trapping supplies.*

Rabbiting with dogs about 1880. The rabbit catcher is holding a ferret spade.

ready to haul it from the net.

Ferreting has always been a favoured way of taking rabbits, being both cheap and silent. Under cover of darkness the ferrets were carried to the warren in the poacher's pocket, a hessian sack or a purpose-built ferret box. Here the poacher set to work covering the burrow exits with *purse nets.* He then put the ferret into the burrow through a net. The ferret bolted the rabbit from the hole into the purse net, where it was quickly dispatched by the poacher. That is how it worked in theory, and usually in practice, but on occasions the ferret harried the hapless rabbit into a dead-end tunnel. When this happened the ferret usually killed the rabbit below ground and remained there gorging itself. The poacher then had to decide whether to abandon his precious accomplice or to stay and dig it out at the risk of being apprehended by the keeper.

Narrow-headed spades, often having long handles with a hook at the tip, were used to dig out ferrets. This hook could be used, if the burrow were straight, to drag out the rabbit carcase, in the hope that the ferret would follow. Another cunning way of doing this was to wheedle a dog-rose briar down the hole, twisting it until it became entangled in the fur of the rabbit, enabling it to be dragged out. Failing this, a *line ferret* was often sent down. This was a ferret with a thin line attached to a collar on which was a small bell. The sound of the bell could be followed underground until the ferret came upon its colleague and the dead rabbit, where it stopped, indicating the exact spot where the poacher should dig to recover both. To eliminate the problem of killing below ground many poachers fitted metal or leather muzzles to their ferrets, and some even went so far as to snap off the ferret's canine teeth with pliers.

Many rabbits were taken with the gun and by the poacher's dog.

Country folk were often loath to hunt hares as it was a widely held belief that they were witches' familiars and could only be shot by a bullet moulded from a silver threepenny piece. The less super-

9

Rabbiting with ferrets in the early years of the twentieth century.

A rabbit bolted by ferrets into a purse net.

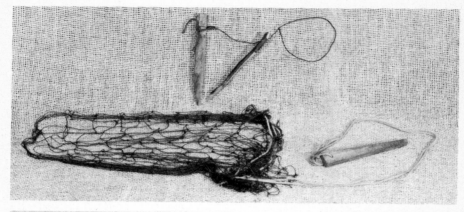

TOP: *A rabbit snare in set position attached to its peg (left) and held in position by the more slender cleft-topped teeler, and (below) a purse net used in ferreting.*

ABOVE: *A ferret spade with a hook at the tip of the haft for extracting a rabbit carcass killed by ferrets below ground.*

stitious, however, used other ways of taking them. A favourite ploy of shepherds, who did their fair share of poaching, was to approach the form (nest) of a hare, already known to them. A short distance from the form the shepherd would stop and bid his dog to bide. He then walked off in a wide circle to come up stealthily behind the hare, whose gaze was concentrated on the dog some distance in front. The shepherd would then strike the unsuspecting hare a sharp blow across the nape of its neck with his crook.

Gate nets were even more widely used for hares than for rabbits, as hares almost invariably chose to duck under a gate to effect their escape when put up by a dog. Hares were also coursed by one or two dogs, usually lurchers or whippets, but two large dogs tearing across a field after a hare were rather conspicuous, so poachers wishing to avoid confrontation with the keeper seldom used this method. Terrier-type dogs were used to put up hares for the gun, the poacher relying on a speedy departure before the arrival of the keeper to investigate the shot. Hares were also commonly taken with snares set on their regular runs.

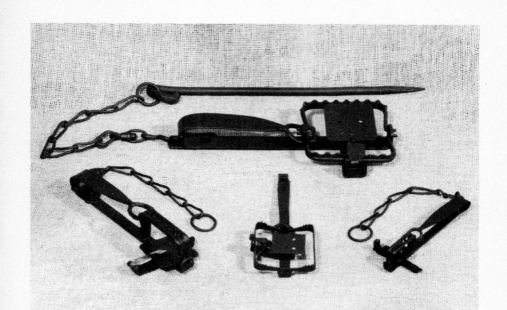

ABOVE: *Steel-toothed or gin traps: (top) a fox trap in set position; (left) a rabbit gin; (centre and right) small ground vermin gins in set and sprung positions.*

BELOW: *Badger gin trap (top) and (below) a smooth-jawed otter trap.*

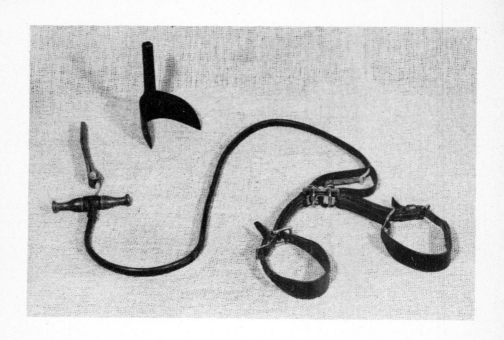

ABOVE:*A hound rounding iron (top left), with a double coursing slip leash.*
BELOW LEFT: *A ferret carrying box.*
BELOW RIGHT: *A trapper's hammer.*

14

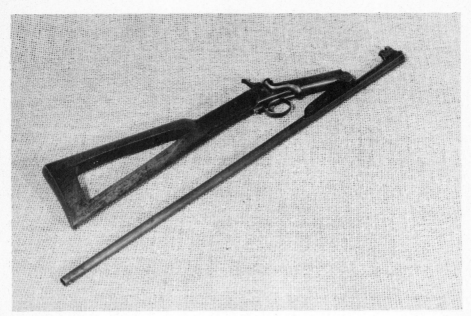

A folding .410, an ideal poacher's gun, easily concealed about the person.

ABOVE: *A telescoping salmon gaff, with steel shaft, brass barrel and turned boxwood handle.*

BELOW: *A mid eighteenth-century muzzle-loading rabbiting gun, complete with ramrod, cleaning rod, shot and powder flasks and tin of paper wads.*

ABOVE: *Partridge or game kites. The lower example is in folded position. The small triangular pouches below the upper kite are stabilising socks.* BELOW: *A simple pheasant trap constructed from hazel rods.*

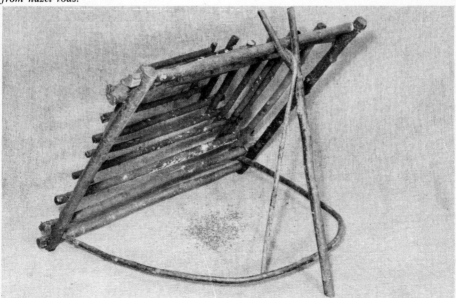

A gamekeeper's hut, doubling as a gibbet, on which he has macabrely hung the victims of his vermin control, predominantly weasels, stoats, crows and magpies.

PHEASANTS AND PARTRIDGES

The partridge has been considered a tasty dish since time immemorial, but the introduction and subsequent intensive rearing of pheasants for estate shoots proved an unparalleled bonanza for the poacher. Vast numbers were raised in pens tended by the keeper and, when released into the coverts, were so accustomed to human presence that they did not flee from the poacher.

A favourite instrument used by the poacher against many small creatures was the *throwing stick*. Generally about 16 inches (400mm) in length, these sticks had a narrow shaft widening into a bulbous head. They were normally carved from a heavy wood such as box or blackthorn and

were often weighted with lead. They were thrown with great accuracy, requiring acute coordination of hand and eye. One of their commonest uses was against roosting pheasants. The poacher crept through the woods at twilight looking up through the branches until he spotted the silhouette of a roosting pheasant; then with a practised flick of his wrist, the throwing stick dislodged the unwary bird from its perch, and both fell into the poacher's arms. Many pheasants were also whisked from their perches by a slender noose of horsehair attached to the end of a thin stick. The common catapult also had a place in the poacher's armoury and was used against roosting pheasants. Like the throwing stick and horsehair noose it was cheap, very effective in practised hands and, above all, silent.

A favourite ploy of many poachers was the *pheasant fence.* This was a very productive way of taking pheasants but had the disadvantage of having to be prepared the evening before the catch, risking its possible discovery by the keeper during the intervening day. The poachers (there would normally be at least two for this operation) erected a fence of interlaced sticks some 3 feet (900mm) high across the width of a coppice, at intervals leaving gaps at ground level large enough to admit a pheasant. In each they set a snare attached to a thin sapling, bent down and pegged. The trap was now set. The following night, accompanied by their dogs, the poachers moved slowly through the copse gently rattling the undergrowth. The essence of this exercise was to create enough motion to disturb the birds but not panic them into flight. The darkness also helped to keep the birds running on the ground. The poachers gently progressed through the copse, the birds scuttling in front until they were confronted by the branchwood fence. Desperately searching for a way through, they found the gaps as the poachers intended. The triggers were touched, the saplings sprang up, the nooses tightened. The poachers collected their bag, reset the snare and repeated the operation from the other end of the copse.

A type of trap used mainly by keepers to catch pheasants for breeding pens resembled an upturned basket constructed of thin hazel rods. It tapered towards the top, where there was a small trap-door which could be opened to remove the trapped pheasant. It was propped open on one side by a thin hazel wand bent through a forked hazel prop so that its lower end lodged behind a hazel bow which was bent in an arc between the two bottom corners near ground level. Grain was scattered within this arc. On its way to the grain the pheasant trod on the hazel bow, depressing it and so releasing the hazel wand. This allowed the cage to drop, confining the bird alive.

Many pheasants succumbed to the poacher's folding ·410 shotgun and a few to the gin trap.

The partridge is such a wily creature that approach is difficult. It whirs suddenly into flight and drops out of sight behind a hedgerow, almost before a gun can be raised. The poacher often used a rather conspicuous aid to help him approach these birds more closely. This was called a *partridge kite, game kite* or *hawk kite* and was shaped to appear like a hawk in flight. This device was flown by the poacher's accomplice over a field known to contain a covey of partridges. Seeing the silhouette of a hawk above, their natural reaction was to 'freeze' close to the ground, relying on their cryptic coloration to protect them and realising too late that a human predator was upon them.

Another method of catching partridges, used on ploughed land, was to set steel-toothed traps in as many furrows as possible and then to advance up the field rattling a can of stones. The partridges ran along the furrows ahead of the poacher, falling victim to the traps. Poachers' dogs hunted partridges through undergrowth and an unpleasant device was used to solve the problem of dogs' ear flaps becoming torn by thorns. Called the *hound rounding iron,* this instrument resembled a stonemason's bolster chisel except that it had a broad horseshoe-shaped blade, which was surmounted by a short steel shaft. The dog's ear flap was placed on a wooden block and this implement was placed on it and given a sharp blow with a wooden mallet, cleanly severing the flap and leaving it neatly rounded. This device mercifully became obsolete by the mid nineteenth century.

Decoy cage traps used to catch small songbirds.

SONGBIRDS

The trapping of songbirds was widespread in the eighteenth and nineteenth centuries. Members of the finch and thrush families were caught for the cage, but blackbirds and thrushes along with sparrows, starlings, larks and others were also taken for the pot.

A great institution for many generations, particularly in the East End of London, has been the 'singing competitions'. Chaffinches, goldfinches, linnets and other finches were caught in their thousands on the marshes and in the woods around London to provide songsters for these competitions. Sometimes they were crossed with canaries to produce 'mules', thought by many to be superior singers. Birds that did consistently well in these competitions commanded high prices, so competition was keen. The best

birds had a following such as a successful racehorse might have today. At these competitions, normally held in upstairs rooms of public houses, each bird was housed in its singing cage, covered with a cloth. Two cages were hung side by side on the wall. Then the covering was removed and both contestants proceeded with their song. Each contestant was judged on the number of 'limbs' it completed over a period of ten minutes, a limb being a full song with an identifiable ending. One bird would often so dominate the other that it silenced it completely. All this took place amidst heavy wagering.

Birds were caught for this trade in many ingenious ways. One of the simplest was *birdlime*, which is any sticky substance used to catch birds. Birdcatchers usually prepared their own lime using a mixture of the residues from boiled holly bark and mistletoe berries, which formed a glutinous substance. This was spread on the twigs of bushes. Seed was spread around, and a *call bird* (a caged bird of the species desired to be caught) was hung nearby. Birds seeing the seed and hearing the calls of their compatriot would alight on the limed twigs. When attempting to take off again their flight feathers would become inextricably glued to the twig. The birdcatcher had only to come along later and pick the birds off the bush. A sophistication of this method was for the birdcatcher to carry with him a sheath full of twigs or brush bristles ready coated with lime. The twigs, cleft or hollowed at the end, were fixed to bushes, while the bristles were stuck into the seedheads of teasels or some other favourite food plant, and they could be used time and again.

Lime was also used in another way to take chaffinches. Dummy male chaffinches were placed out and a call bird was secreted nearby in its cage. The call bird began singing, issuing a threat to the wild chaffinch in its territory. The wild chaffinch would respond by diving to attack the dummy believed responsible for the song. It always flew in from the rear to strike its adversary behind the neck. Just behind the dummy, directly in its flight path, the wily birdcatcher had placed a limed bristle. The chaffinch brushed this with his wings, became entangled and was quickly gathered up. This method was known as 'pegging' a chaffinch.

Nets of all kinds were used to take small birds. Extremely fine *mist nets* were erected vertically to enmesh flying birds. *Clap nets* were also erected vertically but these were baited with seed and a tethered call bird, known as a *brace bird,* and were designed to collapse on the birds when a trigger string was pulled by the concealed catcher. The 'braced' call bird was not confined in a cage but was fitted with a tiny harness made of glove leather, attached, by means of a swivel, to a light line which restrained it. It sat beneath the net on a *flirt stick,* a thin twig from which a line ran to the concealed catcher. The brace bird had enough freedom of movement to hop to the ground and back to the flirt stick. When a flock of finches approached the net the catcher pulled the line, gently raising the flirt stick, then at the right moment dropping it, causing the brace bird to flutter its wings as though it were alighting on the ground. Attracted by this movement, the flock would descend next to it to feed. The catcher pulled the trigger string, collapsing the net on top of them.

Decoy cage traps were commonly employed. These were simple wood and wire cages divided into sections. One section, complete with perch and containers for food and water, housed the decoy bird. The rest of the cage was divided into one, two or three trapping sections, each fitted with a spring-loaded door, which was propped open by a *trigger perch.* Teasel or some other bait was placed inside. The lure of this, combined with the singing decoy, attracted the bird, which, when it alighted on the trigger, sprang it, allowing the door to drop, thus confining itself. Many decoy birds were barbarically blinded by piercing the pupil of the eye with a thin hot needle, as it was believed they would sing more readily in this callously inflicted darkness.

Roosting songbirds were caught at night by means of a *back net.* This was a fine net, supported on two poles in the manner of a protesters' banner. It was held in front of ivy or a wall-climbing shrub where birds were known to roost. The foliage was then shaken and the birds flew blindly into the net. Alternatively it was used on open hedgerows. The net was again held against one side of the hedge, and the bushes were shaken. With this method, however, a man with a lantern stood behind the net. The disturbed birds would fly headlong towards the light into the waiting net.

Spring clap nets with baited trigger platforms were used to take single birds, as also were simple *deadfall traps.* These were often no more than a house brick propped on a twig and baited with seed. This type was only suitable for catching birds intended for the pot.

Another ingenious device for taking birds for the pot was the *lark lure.* It was simply a thin pole stuck in the ground and topped by a revolving wooden head, carved to produce numerous facets. Each of these was studded with tiny mirrors. The head was revolved on its pole by a man concealed some distance away pulling strings,

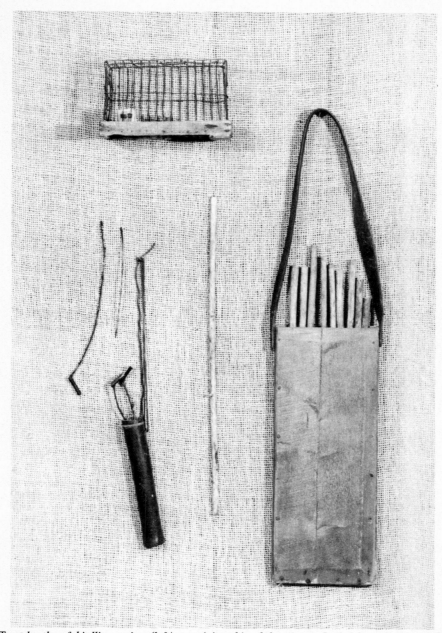

Two sheaths of birdlime twigs: (left) containing thin cleft twigs and whalebone bristles; (right) containing elder twigs with the pith hollowed out. (Top) A decoy cage 7 inches (177mm) long used in conjunction with them.

or in some examples by the breeze. The mirrors, catching the sunlight, glinted, and larks, compelled by their natural curiosity, were attracted to the spot from far afield, presenting ideal targets for the waiting gun.

ABOVE: *A multi-mirrored lark lure.*
BELOW: *A spring clap trap used against small birds, particularly sparrows.*

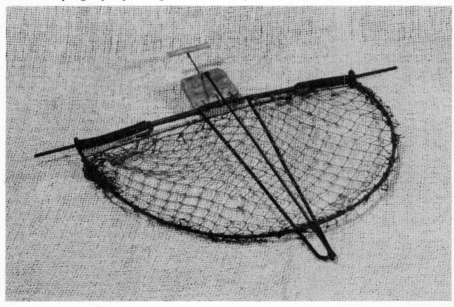

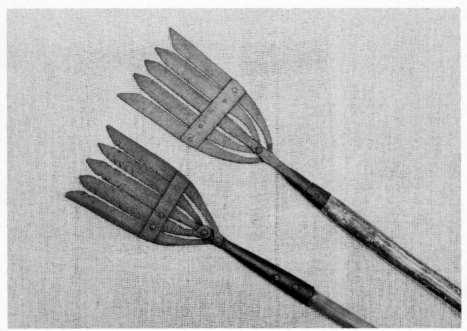

Eel spearheads: two hand-forged early nineteenth-century examples.

EELS, PIKE, TROUT AND SALMON

Eels were a widely caught and nutritious source of food to the working countryman. Their skin also provided a tough, resilient 'leather', with many uses, such as hinges and flail loops. *Legering* was a favourite method of taking them. A weighted line with multiple hook baited with worms was left overnight attached to a thin willow wand stuck in the bank. It was the frailty of this wand that was the key to success. The eel is powerful and tenacious and capable of snapping all but the toughest lines but could gain no leverage against the pliant wand to stress the line. In the morning it would still be hooked, to the delight of the poacher.

Eel spears were also frequently used. These were implements with a head comprising normally four or five flat-

tened, barbed prongs set closely together and mounted on a wooden haft that could be from 5 feet to 20 feet (1.5m to 6m) long, depending on where it was used. The eel spearer prowled the banks of a stream or dyke looking for the tell-tale bubble of the eel. He would then thrust his spear into the mud hoping to bring it out with the eel lodged in its barbs.

An ingenious East Anglian method of catching eels was the *sniggle and batt*. The sniggle was a slender pole some 4 to 5 feet (1.2m to 1.5m) long with a 2-inch (50mm) spike at one end. The batt was a more sturdy piece of wood, some 3 feet 6 inches (1.1m) long, with a broad, club-like head. A succulent worm was impaled on the spike of the sniggle and it was manoeuvred to a position where it wriggled enticingly

23

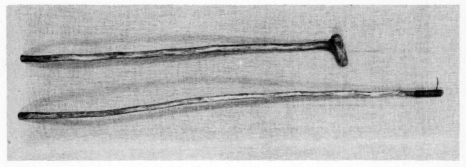

Sniggle (below) and batt, an eel-poaching device from Norfolk.

just over a spot where an eel was known to lurk. As the eel struck to take the worm, the batt was brought sweeping down with speed and force to catch it behind the head, impaling its gullet on the spike of the sniggle. The batt held the eel on the spike as it was hauled from the water.

Eels were also taken in *funnel traps* made of osiers or wire netting, as were many other fish. These, as the name suggests, were simply funnels through which the fish swam into a cage from which it could not return.

Pike, known as 'jacks' in many areas, were frequently taken with a noose of copper wire attached to the end of a long slender pole. The pike was located idling in the water. The poacher assessed its girth and adjusted his noose accordingly. Dropped gently into the water some distance upstream, it was allowed to flow with the current down towards the unsuspecting pike, appearing to it like any other piece of debris being carried downstream. Just in front of his quarry the poacher finally manoeuvred the noose to encircle its body and glide down to a point just in front of its pelvic fins. With a sudden jerk the noose was tightened about the body and the fish was hoisted on to the bank. Many an idling pike has also been skewered with a four-grained dung prong or pitchfork.

Eels and pike filled many an empty stomach, but for those who knew an outlet it was the speckled trout and spawning salmon that filled the pocket. Netting was the most widely used method of taking both. The net was spread from bank to bank and moved gently up river.

Over the years trout tickling has become something of a legend, but it was a practised art which accounted for many fine fish. The tickler knew where to locate the largest fish, hovering almost motionless against the current in a deep recess under the overhanging bank.The hand gently but deliberately entered the water and glided towards the alerted fish. The fingers gently went under the fish's belly; slightly alarmed, the trout began to edge backwards. A little more the fingers stroked; a little more the fish edged back, until the gills were above the fingers. At that moment the tickler struck, grasping the gills with practised fingers and flicking the hapless fish on to the bank.

A favoured way of illicitly taking salmon was the *gaff*. There were many designs, but basically it was a 3 foot 6 inch (1.1m) shaft surmounted by a large hook, sometimes barbed, and normally some 3 to 4 inches (75 to 100mm) across. Some had telescoping shafts which folded away to be carried undetected in the coat pocket. Others had detachable heads connected to a line, which was only fitted to the shaft just before use, so that the stick aiding the rambler through the wood might be the shaft of a gaff awaiting reunion with the head secreted somewhere about his person. The gaff was normally used at the base of a weir, where salmon, exhausted by repeated attempts to leap, idled recuperating in shallow water. The gaff would flash out, the point plunging into the fish and hoisting it ashore. It was quickly dispatched and thrust under the coat of the poacher, who rapidly made his escape.

Two early 'humane' rodent traps, the Everitt (left) and the Sawyer.

VERMIN

Rats and mice have always been the keenest competitors of man, living with him under his own roof and waxing fat from his industry. Man domesticated the cat to combat them, and to its assistance brought many cunningly contrived aids.

Amongst the earliest of these were *deadfall traps*. These were multifarious in design but the basic principle was a heavy weight of stone, wood or metal suspended above a baited trigger platform, which, when sprung, fell on to the victim, crushing it. These were in use until Victorian times.

Cage traps were widely used, these too varying greatly in design. Many worked on the funnel principle already described for the fish trap. Others had spring-loaded doors triggered from a baited platform within; some of these were multiple-catch traps so designed that only the combined weight of numerous animals feeding at once would spring the trap. Some were made of wood, but many of wire or metal to prevent the mouse or rat from gnawing its way to freedom.

Conversely there was another trap called the *guillotine* or *snap-shot* which relied on the mouse's tendency to gnaw to trap it. It was in the form of a box with either three or four mouse-sized holes in one side. At the rear of these holes the bait was placed. Then two strands of thread were pulled across each hole barring access to the bait. These threads also held down a spring-loaded wire noose in each hole. The mouse, gnawing through the thread to reach the bait, released the noose, which crushed it against the roof of the hole.

Another variation on the cage trap was the *seesaw trap*. It was a long box, open at one end, baited at the other. Inside was a simple seesaw, tailored to fit the box exactly. Seeking the bait, the mouse walked the seesaw, tipping it at its point of balance and reaching the bait. Repleted, it scurried back up, but the seesaw did not tip, for a small sprag had dropped, propping up the outward end, which now formed a closed door barring the mouse's escape.

Snares and small gin traps were used to catch rats, as was the *Everitt trap*. This was a metal spring trap similar in some ways to the gin. It had a spring arm and a trigger plate to hold it down, but in place of the hinged jaws were two prongs some 3 inches (75mm) apart. Above these prongs and the trigger plate was a metal arch forming a tunnel, through which the rat ran. Upon being released the prongs sprang upward, pinning the rat to the roof of the arch.

A simple but effective home-made device for taking rats was the *barrel trap*. The head was cut from an ordinary barrel and replaced to pivot on two dowelling studs. A wire spike was fixed to the centre of the head, and the bait was impaled on it. The barrel was then half-filled with water. Any rat treading on the barrel head in attempting to reach the bait tilted it, plunging itself into the water.

Rats were frequently hunted with terriers and occasionally with ferrets.

The mole is an innocuous creature but has for long incurred the wrath of countryfolk by producing its unsightly 'heaves' in pasture and garden. Of necessity the mole must be caught below the ground in its run. These runs are readily detectable to the experienced trapper. The commonest type of mole trap was probably the *pinch-back,* a pincer-like device with double-pronged steel jaws held open in the set position by a small metal trigger plate. It was inserted into the ground so that the jaws rested on either side of the mole's run, and the trigger plate blocked the run. The earth was replaced around the head of the trap, care being taken that none fouled the jaws, whilst the handles, containing the spring, projected above the surface. By attempting to force aside the trigger plate, the mole released the jaws. The trapper could tell by the position of the handles above ground whether or not the trap had been sprung.

Barrel and *half barrel traps* were two alternative types. They relied on catching the mole with wire snares below the ground. The barrel was a hollow wooden cylinder attached to which was a metal spring arm. When set, the head of the arm was held down close to the top of the barrel by a string loop passing through a hole in the barrel's upper surface and retained by a wooden peg inside. When the trap was in this position a wire loop at either end of the barrel was running along a groove carved on the inside surface. The device was carefully inserted into the mole run so that the hollow barrel formed an integral part of it, with the spring arm above the ground. The mole dislodged the peg, releasing the spring arm, which flew up, tightening one of the nooses around its body. The half barrel traps, many home-made, were essentially the same in operation, but the cylinder was replaced by a flat or convex platform, with two metal or wooden hoops below to house the nooses. In home-made examples the spring arm was often a hazel or willow twig.

Another device was the *Anglo Impassable* or steel-spiked mole trap. It was a vertical oblong metal frame with the side sections extended to form two pointed legs, which stuck into the ground. This frame housed a metal rod sheathed in a long spring. At its bottom this bar was attached to a platform containing six 4 inch (100mm) downward-facing spikes. In the set position the spiked platform was pulled up the frame, compressing the spring. It was held set by a niche in a flat metal arm engaging the platform. This pushed a small metal trigger plate, between the legs, into a down position. The trap was then placed in position with the trigger in the run. The mole, pushing up the trigger, disengaged the arm from the platform, allowing the spring to force the spikes down, impaling it. This form of trap was unpopular with many molecatchers as it damaged the pelts, which were at one time much in demand by furriers, providing a lucrative sideline for some country folk.

Many larger birds were considered pests that had to be eradicated — birds of prey and members of the crow family in particular. One of the most common ways of taking these was with the *pole trap,* which was very similar in design to the gin trap except that its base was circular, its jaws crescent-shaped, and the spring arm cunningly modified to a curve following the contours of the base. The reason for its circular shape was that it was set on top of gateposts and poles, favourite perching places for crows and birds of prey. Some had 'clean' and some serrated jaws. Most had flat trigger platforms, but some, specifically designed to catch crows, had a platform shaped to hold a hen's egg. They

ABOVE: *Two seesaw traps: (left) the Claudius trap for weasels; (right) the Premier trap for mice.*

BELOW: *Mole traps: (from left to right) full barrel mole trap; the spiked Anglo Impassable; spring-jawed pinch-back; home-made half barrel.*

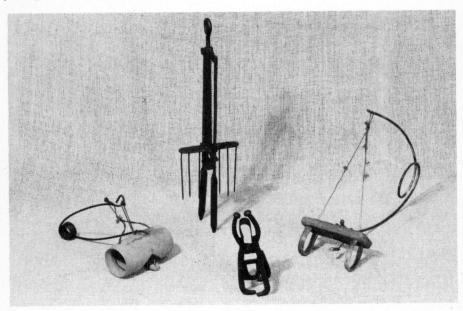

27

Pole traps. The large trap is from Scotland and it was used against golden eagles. The left-hand one has a trigger-platform designed to hold an egg, suggesting its use against members of the crow family. On the right is a hawk or owl trap and in the foreground a tiny pole trap, about 2 inches (50mm) across, used against the kingfisher.

came in a range of sizes; one of the smallest was for the kingfisher, which was considered to be a pest because it took many immature trout and salmon. Fine nets weighted with lead were stretched across streams, also to take this charming little bird. Hawks were also frequently taken in *decoy clap traps*. These traps were in two sections, the lower containing a live decoy, the upper being two semicircular framed nets held open by a trigger device. The hawk, alighting on to the trigger in pursuit of the decoy, brought the two nets snapping together.

Weasels, stoats and otters also faced a policy of extermination, as they 'poached' the precious game. They were mainly taken by shooting, or with snares or gin-type traps. To catch stoats and weasels

these were almost always set in crevices in walls or in artificially constructed tunnels, taking advantage of these animals' habit of hunting in such places. Otters were frequently taken in wire cage traps baited with fish and in gin-type traps.

Foxes and badgers fell most widely to the snare, the gin and the gun. Badgers were, until the nineteenth century, commonly 'dug' for the debased spectacle of badger baiting. Even when you had reached him in his sett this powerful, determined creature was very difficult to extricate, being more than a match for a brace of terriers when cornered. To aid this task a sturdy pair of callipers called *badger tongs* was used to grasp it around the neck and restrain it.

(Left and right) Two Victorian cage mousetraps; (centre) a spring-noose Snapshot mousetrap, 5 inches (127mm) long.

A swivelling spring gun. The trip lines were run from the rings on the rod running horizontally beneath the gun.

THE HUNTER HUNTED

It was the deeply held conviction of all serious poachers that the trout in the brook, the pheasant in the covert, the rabbit in its warren were the property of no one until caught. Unfortunately landowners, gamekeepers and constables did not share that view. So the poacher pursued his quarry with one eye looking back over his shoulder, and his ear strained to catch a sound that betrayed the presence of another abroad in the woods.

If caught unawares few poachers would surrender meekly but would make a run for it, hoping to shake off their pursuer, knowing he needed to apprehend them physically and seize their prey as evidence. The poacher's versatile lurcher dog would often be trained to aid his escape by scampering around a pursuer's legs to impede him. Poacher's dogs were almost always trained to make straight for home should they become separated from their master. If the poacher made good his escape, the keeper would also make straight for his home, hoping to catch him red-handed, arriving with his catch. Few

poachers fell for this and the spoils would be concealed somewhere to be collected later when the danger was over.

Disposing of the products of a night's work could present problems. The flesh could be consumed quickly enough and with relish, but pheasant feathers drifting across a vegetable patch would soon be spotted by the keeper seeking evidence. Villagers often awoke to the acrid stench of feathers and rabbit paunch being burnt in someone's wash-house boiler grate. The antlers and viscera of a deer could be a more substantial problem. These were often disposed of down wells, water being drawn for some time from the well of an understanding neighbour, plied with a few cuts of 'black mutton', as illegally taken venison was often called.

The keeper was not above resorting to methods to combat the poacher which to us today seem barbaric. The *man trap*, in essence a giant gin trap, with heavily toothed jaws up to 2 feet 6 inches (760mm) in length, was frequently set near stiles and on pathways, snapping shut to im-

An eighteenth-century man trap.

A gamekeeper's alarm gun. The trip line was attached to the brass pin retaining the topmost iron weight.

prison the leg with crippling force. Some later models had 'clean' jaws, i.e. without teeth, and were held shut by a lock at each end, to which the keeper held the keys.

Spring guns came in various forms. Perhaps the commonest was mounted on a pivot; it had no butt, a wooden stock, and a short, flared muzzle. Trip-wires were run from it at various angles in such a way that anyone fouling one would swivel the gun in his direction, simultaneously firing it and peppering himself with shot. A variation was a type reminiscent of a small cannon set beside a pathway with the trip-wire set across it. When sprung, this type fired a 4 inch (100mm) iron bolt at the intruder's legs. The use of man traps and spring guns was outlawed in 1829.

Alarm guns were in widespread use. The usual pattern was an iron stake stuck in the ground. On this were mounted, at the lower end, an immovable base plate, and, at the upper end, a short iron chamber with a firing pin projecting from its base. This was loaded with a blank cartridge and held in place by a pin inserted through the stake. From this ran a trip-wire. When sprung, the pin was pulled out, allowing the chamber to slide down the stake. The firing pin, striking the base plate, fired the cartridge, alerting the keeper to the poacher's presence.

Despite all these devices, the persistent harassment by keepers and the harsh penalties faced if apprehended, poaching remained rife. In the words of an old gamekeeper, 'a good poacher is as clever as a keeper, and a little bit more — he has to be.'

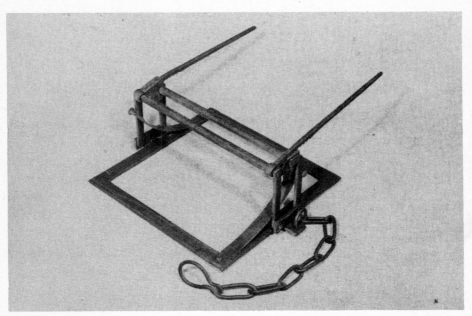

ABOVE: *An early nineteenth-century 'humane' man trap which locked when sprung. The key would be kept by the gamekeeper.*

BELOW: *A spring gun, which fired the iron bolt (alongside it) at the intruder's legs.*

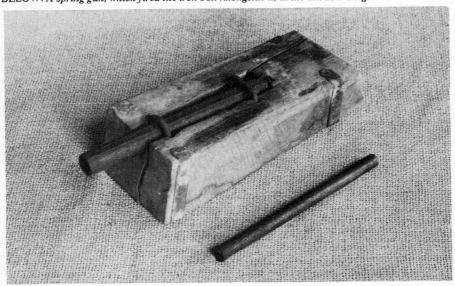

The gamekeeper.